Accessing Heaven By Faith

Dr. Linda K. Smith

Copyright © 2012-2014 Free Them Ministries, Inc.

All rights reserved.

ISBN: 0966338472
ISBN-13: 978-0-9663384-7-8

DEDICATION

This book is dedicated to Patricia King.

In 2010, at a Glory School, Patricia King suggested I write a book about accessing Heaven by faith. I began to tackle the project, but that was the wrong approach. *Tackling* would have been in my own ability and intellect. In fact, the original file I tackled is lost in the mysterious interior of my computer.

I began again and actually found that I had, indeed, begun this task, but in 2008! I think God has been telling me for some time to write this book.

I'm thankful that God has revealed that I must write primarily by revelation and inspiration from Holy Spirit, with the Word of God as the standard.

So I now pray, Father God, by your Holy Spirit, guide my thoughts as I begin to write. Grant to me your divine revelation that I may impart to the readers what you want to tell them about approaching you and your Heaven Realm. I pray in the name of Jesus. Amen

CONTENTS

ACKNOWLEDGMENTS vi

1 GLORY REVEALED 9

2 BY FAITH 13

3 MY GARDEN 19

4 THE MOUNTAIN, THE MIST AND MOSES 23

5 OTHER COUNTRIES 29

7 WHY IS THIS HERE? 35

9 HEAVENLY PROVISION 41

10 WHAT DOES HEAVEN LOOK LIKE? 45

11 CLOUD OF GLORY 51

12 WHERE IS HEAVEN? 53

13 THE MEAL OF MANNA 57

14 YOUR TURN 59

ACKNOWLEDGMENTS

I wish to personally thank the following people for their contributions to my inspiration and knowledge and other help in creating this book:

Patricia King for the concept and encouragement to write this book.

Robert Smith for the vision to provide ISBN numbers years before I started producing books.

Patricia Harrington for 'exposing' me to the outer limits of faith.

INTRODUCTION

Heaven and Earth, Earth and Heaven, Heaven on Earth, on Earth as it is in Heaven. Two realms existing simultaneously yet earth does not exist without coming out of Heaven and here we are caught between the two.

I used to be heavenly minded yet earth bound. I knew there was a heaven but never went there in the Spirit realm, by faith. I knew we wanted Heaven on earth yet it seemed like work to get it to manifest.

This book is presented in an unusual format. That's ok, Heaven is not usual, it is supernatural. The apostle Paul felt this dichotomy. He wanted to be with Christ, but knew he had service to do on earth, service to the Lord.

I understand the emotions of Paul. I too want to be in Heaven more than on earth. However, it thrills me to serve my Lord and my God daily until the time comes for Him to change my location eternally.

The chapters of this book alternate between Heaven and Earth. It is my desire that my visions and heavenly experiences will 'prime the pump' for you. And I trust that the revelation in the Word which God and wonderful teachers have imparted to me will aid and expand your understanding of what you will experience.

The Bible does not restrict our heavenly experience unless we wield it legalistically outside of loving relationship with Christ. So I pray you read about Heaven with joy and study the scriptures with love.

DR LINDA K SMITH

1 GLORY REVEALED

John 3:12
If I have told you earthly things, and ye believe not,
how shall ye believe,
if I tell you of heavenly things?

The room is dimmed; just soft light playing off the walls. The instrumental music is melodic, reflective, sometimes stirring as it floats across my hearing. I close my eyes and cause my body and soul to quiet. Be still.

My breathing slows, I feel all stress slide away. Stray thoughts of worldly obligations try to break in. Go away. Be still.

My hearing notices ambient noise from the air conditioner, the traffic outside. Pay attention. Be still.

Finally, after too many minutes wasted, I enter in. Where is this? Heaven! Where in Heaven? I begin to allow exploration. I see colors; colors that seem to be lit from within, almost neon in characteristic. Neon is not the right word. They are . . . alive! There are the primary and secondary colors of red, green and blue. They swirl and flow against the inky blackness of the universe.

I encounter the brightest white, the most majestic purple, brilliant yellow and gold, blending yet separate. I seem to be moving through the sky, but without an intended destination, allowing Holy Spirit to select the route.

The colors are gone and I stand before two massive doors. Surely, whatever, whoever is behind these is very important. The doors open on their own volition. I walk, no, glide through. My peripheral vision lets my mind know the room is glorious with an atmosphere of some sort for a ceiling and light that does not come from a lamp or candle.

I am aware that the music still plays. If I choose, I can still hear the ambient noise. I choose not to hear.

This heavenly, majestic room becomes secondary to what fills my 'vision' now. I see The Throne, God's Throne! I bow, but still continue gliding toward The Throne as if drawn by a power not my own. Holy, holy, holy. Be still.

I sense, I know 'He' is on the throne. Father. God. Creator. I Am. Though there seems to be no form, I know my God is there. As I bow lower, I sense I'm at His feet. My understanding interrupts.

"John 4:24 says God is Spirit and Jesus said Spirit has not flesh and bones. Why am I sensing Father as a man? Why am I seeing feet?"

No sooner did I think this than Holy Spirit answers. "Be still."

I dare to touch His feet. I feel a hand on my head soft and gentle as a father's loving caress. In subsequent visits He will lift me to His lap. I will feel His heartbeat, but for now, I can only dare to be at His feet. Be still.

I may stay as long as He wants. I may return often. There are divine assignments to be carried out, but for now I know the joy of bowing before His throne.

I have no desire to move away, to know what else is in this room. There's only Him. There's no analysis. There's no logical reasoning.

There's just the reality of being with Him. This is the most real reality I have ever known. There's purity here. There's comfort here. There's peace here.

Time means nothing here for there is no time. Time is part of the ambient environment in which my body sits. Be still. His feet. . . !

Alas, I must 'go back'. Without leaving the room, I am suddenly back in the universe and the colors seem to rejoice. They escort me as I journey to my starting point.

I am back in the room of my earth environment. I open my eyes. I take a deep breath. The music still plays. There's the air conditioner kicking on. A car passes. The peace returned with me. Be still.

DR LINDA K SMITH

2 BY FAITH

Hebrews 11:1
Now faith is the substance of things hoped for,
the evidence of things not seen.

This book could be filled with Biblical references and scriptures about Heaven and we could gain a lot of head knowledge by reading those passages. However, access is by faith and faith alone. As I write those words, I can feel the literal legalists twitching. Yes, Jesus Christ had to make the way for us to have access, but not everyone has faith in the truth of what is available. It's like knowing there is a million dollars in our bank account, but not believing we can spend it freely.

There are many promises in God's word that are never accessed because those who read them or hear about them never choose to believe in them to the point of personally experiencing the greatness of the power of God and the love of the Father.

Heaven is, indeed, a wonderful environment and I enjoy visiting on a regular basis. Those visitations are so real to me. No one can talk me out of the experience. I go because I believe I can go. I go because I choose to believe I have access with boldness according to scripture.[1] My faith provides evidence of the Heaven I cannot see with my natural eyes.[2]

As we approach the end of this age and the return of Christ (no longer on the cross, but now glorified, ascended), there are more and more individuals experiencing Heaven. More than any other time in our history, books are being written, more interviews are being granted, and more documentaries being produced which all give accounts of visits to Heaven.

The stories are amazingly similar though not identical. The differences, I believe, are simply due to the rendition of the person describing his or her experiences. We all 'see' things differently. We tend to describe things in terms familiar to our own understanding.

Heaven is real enough that there are great similarities in all the visitations. One of my favorite books is *Intra Muros* (now titled *Within Heaven's Gates*) by Rebecca Springer. As a theologian, I understand that there are descriptions in the book that don't seem to fit with a literal academic understanding of scripture. But, overall, I cannot read that book without knowing Ms. Springer's experience was absolutely wonderful and has increased my understanding of the bounty and beauty of Heaven.

My mother, who passed away in her eighties, had a wonderful Heavenly experience during her final days which is described in a later chapter.

Another experience was with my brother. He was given three weeks to live due to a form of cancer. He is a believer in God through Christ Jesus. Through faith he lived 3-1/2 years after that diagnosis serving the Lord, leading people to salvation through Jesus Christ.

During his final days, the pain level had grown and in order to overcome it, he had begun to sit for long hours meditating on God and His Kingdom. During these times of meditation, he would

---

[1] Ephesians 3:12
[2] Hebrews 11:1

'travel'. At the time, we did not know about supernatural travel and had no explanation for it although we did know that in scripture people were transported. (Think of Elijah)

He would describe being in another place and it was so real he thought maybe he was actually there. We believed it, not having an explanation, but faith in God's power and ability to do the impossible. My brother passed peacefully in the hospital. I wonder 'where' he was when his spirit left earth.

For the more academic reader, let me now give you some scriptural foundation and I apologize in advance for using King James English, but it is public domain. You may use your own preferred Bible version.

Romans 5:2 By whom also we have access **by faith** into this grace wherein we stand, and rejoice in hope of the glory of God.

Ephesians 2:18 For through him we both have access **by one Spirit** unto the Father.

Ephesians 3:12 In whom we have boldness and access with confidence **by the faith of him**.

The Bible also tells us we are saved by grace through faith. So, if you are saved, if you have faith, can you now believe you have access?

Here's more evidence:

Hebrews 4:16 Let us therefore come boldly unto the throne of grace, that we may obtain mercy, and find grace to help in time of need.

The throne of grace is in Heaven's realm. It must be accessed. Jesus came to earth and His obedience to the death of the cross, and God's power in resurrection and ascension, gave us access. The throne of grace didn't come to earth, Jesus came to earth. However, God in God's matchless love, allowed us to access grace that was available through Heaven.

God has always wanted man to be where God is. God told Moses to 'come up and be here' on the mountain.[3] He told Noah to come into the ark.[4]

I also want you to consider:

2 Corinthians 12:2 I knew a man in Christ above fourteen years ago, (whether in the body, I cannot tell; or whether out of the body, I cannot tell: God knoweth;) such an one caught up to the **third heaven.**

Paul accessed third Heaven! I remember the first time I read this. I thought it was interesting in an academic way and just read past it. I also recall the first time I heard someone present it as a reality that I could achieve. . . by faith. My intellectual mind wanted to reject the idea. Perhaps it was heresy or blasphemy or some such thing. I went back into the Bible and worked it until I understood this portion. It became *rhema*[5] to me. It became a deep personal understandable reality.

By faith, I prayed, "Father I want to experience more of you and all of you. If I can now access third Heaven as Paul did, take me there, but if I should not do so, keep me far from it. In the name of Jesus I pray, amen."

Of course, I immediately began to access third Heaven. I saw vibrant colors unlike those of earth. They enveloped me; greens, blues, purples, reds, whitest white. I began to smell aromas not of this earth. I began to sense activity in the angelic realm. I was able to enter the throne room and lay at the feet of God and then return to my earthly existence. Oh my!

I have revisited many times and now see details of the throne room (if I can tear myself away from the Father for a bit and sometimes God encourages me to explore). I've seen other buildings in Heaven; the Hall of Wisdom for example. I've seen the river

---

[3] Exodus 24:1, 12
[4] Genesis 7:1
[5] Spoken word of God

flowing from the throne. I've seen strategy rooms, and many other areas of that realm.

I've also done battle in the second Heaven where the principalities, powers and dominions are active.[6]

Mark 9:23 Jesus said unto him, If thou canst believe, all things are possible to him that believeth.

Heaven is my home. I'm a citizen of that good land and I can visit anytime I desire to visit.

Philippians 3:20 For our conversation (citizenship) is in Heaven; from whence also we look for the Savior, the Lord Jesus Christ:

The refreshing which I experience with each visit is vital to me. When I return to earth, do I leave the Father? No. Through His Spirit, Father is always with me. I have Christ in me, the hope of glory. Faith is the substance of things hoped for; the evidence of things not seen.

I know you are hoping for Heaven. I know you can't see it with your natural eyes right now. By faith, grab the substance and evidence! Use your spiritual eyes. Your visits now may be shorter than desired and temporary, but God will receive you whenever you exercise your faith to drop by the House.

The more you visit Heaven you will discover Heaven comes back with you. I now smell heavenly smells in my apartment or church at times. I am more aware of angelic activity around me. I have had oil appear on the pulpit when I was preaching. I have seen a mist or rain inside during Christian meetings. And, of course, there is the 'gold dust', the feathers, the gemstones, etc.

You can try to remain skeptical. I once was also skeptical. I pray, like me, your 'wisdom' is overwhelmed by the undeniable manifestation(s) of the power and love of God.

---

[6] Ephesians 2:2, 6:12

3 MY GARDEN

Song of Solomon 4: 12-15
A garden enclosed is my sister, my spouse; a spring shut up, a fountain sealed. Thy plants are an orchard of pomegranates, with pleasant fruits; camphire, with spikenard, spikenard and saffron; calamus and cinnamon, with all trees of frankincense; myrrh and aloes, with all the chief spices: a fountain of gardens, a well of living waters, and streams from Lebanon. Awake, O north wind; and come, thou south; blow upon my garden, that the spices thereof may flow out. Let my beloved come into his garden, and eat his pleasant fruits.

New territory. The preacher said God told Him what Adam lost is restored in Christ and Adam lost access to the Garden. I am, by faith, visiting my Garden.

I shut out distractions, I still my mind and soul. Soaking music, inspired by God is playing in my ears. The vision forms before me. What is this place? A small walled garden appears around me. I am no spectator, but rather exist in this new place.

At first it seems familiar, almost like earth, but more perfect. The air is pure, the light different, not from a blazing sun, but originating in itself. There is grass so green. There are flowers similar to earthly flowers but they seem more alive, as though they are looking at me with joy.

I sit on a nearby bench and listen. The 'sounds' are of peace. This is the sound of heavenly solitude. I gaze at the patch of flowers before me and realize they produce something shiny. Gemstones! Why? It brings Father joy to surprise me in this way.

My mind, so use to the practicalities of earth, wants to know the purpose for everything I see. Be still. Explore. What is on the other side of the walls?

I go through the gate, noticing the intricate design. Before me is what the writers of old called a sward. The grass is a like a lush carpet, soft, pure, gently moving with the breeze. A distance away two chairs. Adirondacks. Why Adirondacks? I would not have chosen them on earth. A small table sets between them. They are waiting for someone. Me? Who else?

I lower myself into one chair. A low wall appears just in the distance. As I look up, towering royal palm trees spring up. Tall and majestic without a conscious thought or desire to have trees. Who ordered these? They are exquisite.

I realize there is no decay anywhere, no wilting, no destructive pest, only beauty. Beyond the low wall more lawn gently flows to the sea. The water is so inviting, no towering waves, no dangerous undertow. A short distance from the shore is a large rock almost the size of a small island. Again, my mind is inquisitive. Be still. Observe.

I rise from the chair and find myself standing on the low wall like a child balancing, arms outstretched. I make the small jump to the grass beyond. The shore beckons. Can I swim to the rock? What is on the other side of the rock? Am I strong enough to make it around the rock?

A familiar voice, without words, laughs softly and tells me I am still thinking in earth terms. Here there is no effort. I can walk through the water if I choose. I can walk through the rock if I choose, or simply *be* on the other side of the rock. Such a strange reality, but real nonetheless.

I am in the sea. The sea welcomes me. On the other side of the rock island. . . more sea. I return to the grassy expanse. I notice the vineyard. Was it there before? The vines seem to be celebrating. They stretch out in neat rows, but free from the restraint of wires as they would have been on earth. I walk down a row and the vines call me to dance. I hear them laughing. I began to twirl. Such joy! Such fun! Grinning, I fall to the ground looking to the sky, then turning my gaze under the vines, across the rows.

Feet approaching! I know those feet. They are the feet of my Lord. I quickly rise to see His face. My breath seems to leave my body. That face!

His robe is stained, no, splashed with juice from the grapes, but the grapes are not crushed. They give their bounty freely, but there is no destruction here. I too feel the nectar on my skin, my lips. Communion.

He laughs and reaches out a beautiful hand to me. We dance through the vines, never tangled for the vines join us in the dance. Marvelous!

DR LINDA K SMITH

4 THE MOUNTAIN, THE MIST AND MOSES

> Exodus 19:16 And it came to pass on the third day in the morning, that there were thunders and lightnings, and a thick cloud upon the mount,

Exodus is more than a Bible story. It's about real people and real events. I believe that truth by faith. A children's pastor in a well-established denominational church in our town told one of our pastors that the Bible was fallible and that the book of Revelation was only a dream. This young pastor had finished seminary, was working in a church teaching our next generation, but had no faith in the very words upon which Christianity is founded!

Your Bible says all scripture is given by inspiration of God (Greek, *theopneustos*, or God-breathed[7]. Though it has gone through some changes over the years, the solid, basic, and infallible word of God is still there.

---

[7] 2 Timothy 3:16

In Exodus God wanted Moses to access Him on a personal level.

Exodus 19:16 And it came to pass on the third day in the morning, that there were thunders and lightnings, and a thick cloud upon the mount, and the voice of the trumpet exceeding loud; so that all the people that was in the camp trembled. [17] And Moses brought forth the people out of the camp to meet with God; and they stood at the nether part of the mount. [18] And Mount Sinai was altogether on a smoke, because the LORD descended upon it in fire: and the smoke thereof ascended as the smoke of a furnace, and the whole mount quaked greatly. [19] And when the voice of the trumpet sounded long, and waxed louder and louder, Moses spoke, and God answered him by a voice. [20] And the LORD came down upon mount Sinai, on the top of the mount: and the LORD called Moses up to the top of the mount; and Moses went up.

Exodus 24: 15-16 And Moses went up into the mount, and a cloud covered the mount. [16] And the glory of the LORD abode upon Mount Sinai, and the cloud covered it six days: and the seventh day he called unto Moses out of the midst of the cloud.

Exodus 33:9 And it came to pass, as Moses entered into the tabernacle, the cloudy pillar descended, and stood at the door of the tabernacle, and the Lord talked with Moses.

Time after time, God called Moses to spend time. We see, throughout the Bible, God in a separate setting than the earth with the exception of God in the flesh in the form of Jesus.

Even in the Garden in Eden, God was in the sanctified place called the Garden. When Adam died and was put out of the Garden, it was the spiritual connection with God in the holy place that died. Separation from the presence of our Heavenly Father feels like death. Accessing Heaven by faith is life.

God spoke to Moses in a cloud. God's glory was seen in the Holy of Holies. God was within the Ark into which he beckoned Noah, but did not let Noah see His presence. Moses had to 'come up' to be in God's presence and God spoke from the mist or the cloud, face to face, but veiled.

Some of you may be thinking of Jacob right now. In Genesis 32 we read of him wrestling with a man and Jacob later said, "I have seen God face to face." I believe Jacob wrestled with an angel of the Lord and saying he saw God face to face is equivalent to saying, "this is of God." I say this because for God to speak to Moses, there was a cloud, a covering. Jacob is no Moses.

Nevertheless, God desires the presence of man for reasons that are still mysterious to me at the moment. Why would God desire to be with us? It must be love.

I will point out that Jacob was alone when this event took place. When we enter the presence of God, accessing Heaven, it is an intensely personal moment though we may be in a crowd. Like Moses, we must be able to sense or hear the invitation of God. We must separate ourselves and we must go up or into a higher and greater dimension.

Notice the emphasis on the presence of the Lord in the following verses:

Genesis 3:8 And they heard the voice of the LORD God walking in the garden in the cool of the day: and Adam and his wife hid themselves from the **presence of the LORD God** amongst the trees of the garden.

Genesis 4:16 And Cain went out from the **presence of the LORD**, and dwelt in the land of Nod, on the east of Eden.

In order to avoid the presence of God we must hide or go out. Therefore, to access the presence of God we must present ourselves to God or go in.

We are addressing, in this book, accessing Heaven by faith. For me, to be in the presence of God is to be in Heaven. I don't see them separately. Heaven is the dwelling place of God. Where God is; that *is* Heaven. Because Christ dwells within us[8], we can experience Heaven on earth.

Did you know that in scripture any place above the ground is referred to as Heaven? The Heaven I am referring to is the dwelling place of God.

The mist or cloud is very significant to deep encounters with God. God is in no way limited by when or how God encounters us. We, however, have certain challenges that come with being in an earthly environment. We can be easily distracted. God wrapped Moses in a cloud in a separate place, thus shutting out distraction.

Think again about Hebrews 11:1. Now faith is the substance of things hoped for; the evidence of things not seen. Faith is not a sensory experience. We believe and then see. By faith, within the cloud, Moses had no need to 'see' anything earthly, but his vision became a supernatural vision within the realm of glory of God.

In my experience, I needed to exercise encountering God by separating myself from the usual environment (some of you might be familiar with the prayer closet model), I had to block my vision from my surroundings and I blocked my hearing as well. It was sort of a form of sensory deprivation. Once external stimulus was quieted, the only thing I had to harness was my thought patterns.

After years of practicing this process, I can now shut out my surroundings without isolating myself, although I require intimate, isolated time with my God. I can access Heaven in a crowd, amid chaos. However, it is still really nice to isolate myself and meet with God privately. As I write this book, I am listening to God-inspired instrumental music. The lights of the room are dim. The phone is silent. No visitors allowed. It's the Godhead and me and the revelation.

Jesus did this from time to time. Paul did this from time to time. Elijah did this. Many others in the Bible and in the Body of Christ

---

[8] Colossians 1:27

have done or do this; getting alone with God. I don't make God come to me. I go to God.

As I review this chapter Holy Spirit is telling me about Daniel in the lion's den.[9] Shut in the den, the only distraction was the enemy, the lions. Daniel could spend this isolation being terrified of the potential attack or he could choose it as an intimate time with God, ignoring the threat. When we come away with God, the threats are still all around us, but we shut them out of our heavenly experience with God. They, the enemies, cannot and must not be allowed to invade.

Sometimes God calls me to meet with Him and when I obey, I am on a mountain top sitting in the mist. I have come to know, for me, this means God desires to teach me something, to impart some revelation. I can, of course get revelation without being on the mountain, but there are times when God wants it this way and I obey.

In the mist, I can sense angels moving around hurriedly, obviously on some assignment having to do with instructing the Church. The lessons learned here have a different 'flavor' than other revelation. They are foundational. They are benchmarks for discernment. I do not possess the words to explain the difference adequately, but I love being called to the mountain in the mist.

---

[9] Daniel 6

5 OTHER COUNTRIES

I am asleep, I think. Except how did I get on this bus? Kenya is beautiful this time of year. The breeze blows through the open windows. It is warm, but not unbearable. Where are my traveling companions? I shouldn't be in Kenya alone.

I hear the unfamiliar words as locals chatter away in the other seats. I hear the cackle of chickens. I hope the driver is careful. This road is busy and Kenyan drivers wreck frequently. We pass small lean-to's where women are hawking their wares, fruit, vegetables, trinkets. There are people on bikes barely missed by the bus as it bumps over the ruts.

We stop at a small building that has no doors or windows. It is just open to the dusty air and heat. I am suddenly inside without any effort of my own.

The people are waiting, sitting on a variety of benches and chairs. Mysteriously a microphone appears. How do they power it in this remote setting? They look at me expectantly.

I began to share the Word of God. I am confident. I sense my divine assignment. A small girl walks with me on my right, holding my hand. She desires impartation. Will she be the one who changes Kenya for the Kingdom? We walk, I preach.

A woman places an infant in the crook of my left hand that holds the microphone. The three of us walk back and forth as the Words pour out.

The 'dream' (vision?) ends.

Back at my home church that I pastor, I am preaching. A family has brought their grand-daughter. So cute, so little. I am preaching, holding a microphone. The tiny girl walks to the front and stands to my right. It's like the dream! She 'preaches' with me, imitating my every movement. I ask a question of the congregation, she answers in the affirmative. She is highly anointed. Will she be the one the change Texas for the Kingdom?

Praise is perfected in the mouth of babes. This is a divine moment, a prophetic moment and she has sensed and obeyed the unction from Holy Spirit. What just happened in the Spirit Realm? I don't know, but something did happen. Something significant happened.

Did God transport me? Did I actually preach in Kenya or was it just a dream. I believe, by faith, I was there.

6 HIGHER WAYS, GREATER THOUGHTS

Isaiah 55:9
For as the Heavens are higher than the earth,
so are my ways higher than your ways,
and my thoughts than your thoughts.

The word 'higher', in the ancient Hebrew means lofty and exalted. God acts and thinks loftily. This passage doesn't say, "And you should keep it that way and not raise your thoughts and methods." God is telling us, if we want to think and act in a more God-like manner, we're going to have to 'step it up'.

This is exactly why Paul said in Ephesians 3:20, " Now unto him that is able to do exceeding abundantly above all that we ask or think, according to the power that works in us."

God does exceedingly abundantly above according to the power that works in us. What power works in you? If it's faith in the power of God, if it's Christ in you, then God will not limit what God does by what you and I ask or think. God goes over and above that because God thinks and acts higher.

What can limit this? Not letting the power work in us limits this. A lack of faith limits this. But the real key we should note in this verse is, 'as the Heavens are higher than the earth'. Accessing Heaven means accessing someplace higher than where we are or more lofty than the earth experience.

Because we are so experienced in the restrictions of earth and human thinking, we want to put everything in a physical mode and think of Heaven as physically 'up'. We lift our faces to the sky looking for God. We think of Heaven as physically beyond the clouds. Perhaps it is, but it is also within us.

Perhaps when God gave the example of Moses coming up to the mountain top to meet with God, we were being shown in a type that we must mentally, emotionally and spiritually ascend to God.

Be curious about Heaven. Be curious about the throne of God. Believe the Word. Believe Heaven is real and the Throne 'Room' exists.

Imagine a child who has no curiosity. Imagine a child lays there with no interest in exploring the world around it. Though the child grows, the child never tries to roll over, walk, talk, doesn't look around and is just not interested in the possibilities which are presented. We would have that child to the doctor as fast as we could get him or her there!

When Moses saw the burning bush, a sight that was most definitely NOT logical, he 'turned aside' to see this marvelous thing. Moses was curious.

God's children need to have a curiosity about the things of God. Daddy God wants us to explore Heaven, the realm of glory, the Throne Room, and more. Avoid being so cynical that you lose your curiosity. You don't have to be so 'grown up' all the time. Play at the feet of God. Ask God questions about Heaven, angels, and glory.

When Jesus prayed for the apostles He said they were in the world, BUT not of the world. Let us not be so earthbound that we can't find Heaven. God is a God of possibilities. If we do not allow our thoughts to ascend out of our carnal realities into the heights of possibilities through Christ, what good work will we ever achieve?

Peter had to have a higher thought than sinking in the sea in order to walk on water. That higher thought came because he saw Jesus walk on water and knew if Jesus could do it, he could try it. Trying to walk on water was the only way to obtain the real experience and victory.

Jesus said He only did what He saw the Father do. The higher thought came from watching the Father. Jesus went on to say that we would do greater works than He did. Since we didn't walk with Him on earth, we must believe by faith He did miracles, signs and wonders in order for us to try to do the greater things. I think we can now begin to understand why the Church has become somewhat anemic in demonstrating the power of God.

I challenge you right now to be very courageous. Put the book down for just a moment and think, "I will access Heaven." Go up and be there. Or think that you really can lay hands on the sick and they will recover or believe that miracles can, do and will happen.

7 WHY IS THIS HERE?

I make the approach once again. The room is dim and quiet. The music plays softly in my ears. In my Spirit, I travel through the Heavens thinking I'll arrive in the Throne Room, but what is this place?

The street is quiet, still. The shops are closed, no, prepared and waiting. What are shops doing in Heaven? I don't understand. For what are they waiting? For whom are they waiting?

The air is crisp and cool but it is not morning or evening. Everything is so clean, not a speck of dust. Even the buildings have an air of expectation. This place is longing for the people of God. Where are they?

My theology is running through scriptures for explanation. New Jerusalem? Would God let me peak at the streets of New Jerusalem? Surely not. . . or maybe.

I walk through the street peering into windows, but I don't move by my own physical effort. I think and therefore move along. The physics are a mix of supernatural and familiar.

Creation groans for the manifestation of the sons (offspring) of God. This place is yearning for us. All of Heaven is looking for the day we join the Father, Son and Holy Spirit forever in the heavenlies. For now they wait except for our infrequent visits.

This place seems whimsical. Will we really care about such things throughout eternity? Is God being playful like a father buying his little girl a doll house? I recall He said come, buy without money.[10] Hmmm.

I have heard others speak of things they have seen in Heaven, things that seemed ridiculous to me. Were they correct or are our experiences in Heaven for a season particular to our experience only?

I must go. I must think. I must ask Father.

---

[10] Isaiah 55

8 BEFORE THE FOUNDATION OF THE WORLD

> Ephesians 1:4
> Even before he made the world,
> God loved us and chose us in Christ
> to be holy and without fault in his eyes.

I was just thinking, again, how being too academic can steal the joy out of the Word and the things of God. What came to mind is how some 'theologians' struggle and argue over the simplest scriptures. The Word is correct that God made the simple things to confound the wise. Many reject the simple truths of predestination and the foreknowledge of God.

Here's the thing that I know by faith. . . God knew me before Genesis 1:1. Whether you want to think as an individual or corporately, God thought of us before God made the earth. It's time we realize that we existed in the spirit realm, in Heavenly places, in the mind of God before we ever were born. You are from Heaven so it should be normal for you to visit or access Heaven from time to time. Do you not visit friends and family here on earth? Well, Heaven is much greater and much more accessible through Christ.

To access Heaven by faith is to access Heaven by love. God is our Father. God loves us. God cares for us. God desires our presence. Jesus is our Lord and brother. We have been adopted into the family of God through God's great love whereby He gave His only begotten Son, Jesus.

Because I absolutely love, love, love God, Jesus, and Holy Spirit, I want to be with them all the time. While I do have Christ in me, the hope of glory, I also know through scripture that Christ is seated at the right hand of God the Father in Heavenly places. Jesus said, "I go to prepare a place for you that where I am there you may be also."

Why, oh why, do we think that's something that should happen only in the future? That's where He is so that's where I am!

When God made Adam and Eve, God made them Spirit BEFORE God made them body and soul. Yes, check it out. God said, "let us make man in our own image." What is the image of God, particularly at that time before Jesus came in the form of a man? John 4:24 says God is a Spirit. Luke 24:39 tells us Spirit has not flesh and bones. After God made Adam, God formed a body and breathed into it soul life.

When you think of the Godhead, God is Spirit, Jesus is body, Holy Spirit is in the body to cause the believer to function in the supernatural.

You and I are more spirit than body and soul. Spirit knows no limitations. I can enter the presence of God, the Throne Room in the Spirit any time. Dare to try it! You and I started out there and we'll end up there. What about in between? I will visit Father God. I can walk freely to the Throne of Grace.

A three year old Christian boy in our church was recently settled down for a nap. Later his mother asked him if he enjoyed his nap. He told her, 'Yes', that he had went flying with Jesus. She asked him what he saw while he was flying. He said he saw purple, and clouds and angels! Children know Heaven is real. It's only when we become adults and someone tells us Heaven is just an allegory that we become jaded to the reality of the Kingdom and our access to the Kingdom including Heaven.

You existed before this planet on which we live, to which we are tied by more than just gravity. In Christ we are free indeed. We are free to believe the Word, free to explore Christian faith, free to access everything God has provided and offered to His children.

Once you begin to exercise faith in this free access, your spiritual experience will multiply exponentially. At first you might just see colors. You might just see clouds. But as you continue, you can travel anywhere in time and space that Holy Spirit leads.

Elijah was transported. Paul was in the third Heaven and couldn't even tell if it was in the body (which must have been possible) or out of the body. Even satan, as read in the book of Job, walked into the presence of God. If satan could do it, God certainly would let God's children come into God's presence!

Heaven is our true homeland. Heaven is where our true citizenship lies. Heaven is where we started out before the foundation of the world. Heaven is our future destination and a great place to visit while we await Christ's return to take us home.

Through Christ, we are restored to a paradise state with the added privilege of being adopted into the family of God. We are not mere creations, we are God's children! Adam walked with God. Adam spent time with God and God sought to spend time with Adam. These were quality times, not just for mundane purposes. These were times of companionship, fellowship.

God still desires time with God's children. God takes pleasure in each of us, delights in our fellowship. You and I are God's workmanship created in Christ Jesus. We are the apple of His eye. Just as Jesus would go to the mountain to be alone with the Father, so must we take the time to do so.

After the fall of Adam we find people trying to access God by their own means when they built the tower of Babel. They were trying to reach into Heaven, but not through relationship. God preserved the way. The language was scattered and not until men and women of God approached God with a pure heart did we see the companionship restored.

God would refer to people as 'a man after my own heart'. David said whether he went to Heaven or Hell, God was there. Why? God wanted to be with David. God offered His presence to David as He did to Adam.

You are part of creation and creation is groaning for the manifestation of the sons of God. Therefore, you have a yearning inside you to manifest as your were created, to be with God.

9 HEAVENLY PROVISION

James 1:17
Every good gift and every perfect gift is from above,
and cometh down from the Father of lights,
with whom is no variableness,
neither shadow of turning.

The Throne Room seems so familiar now. God is about to add to the familiar.

I approach. The Father smiles as if knowing something I have not yet discovered. Father directs my attention to an adjoining room. It is so majestic. Wait, Father, my attention is for You and You alone!

It pleases the Father. He beckons me to explore. I am instructed to enter the antechamber. The finishes are so opulent. The wood columns gleam. The floor is marble or gold or. . . what? It is almost translucent and obviously priceless.

The walls of the antechamber are floor to ceiling drawers and the ceiling is very high! How would I ever reach those drawers. Father tells me to pick a drawer. I still feel my attention should be directed solely at the Father, but I must obey.

How do I choose. Holy Spirit says, "Listen."

My gaze travels to the highest drawer above me and my body follows the thought. Father says to reach inside. I can't see into the drawer. My hand finds an object. I retrieve it. A scepter! It's beautiful! It is metallic blue and crystal. Is this mine? Can I have it? The Father laughs. I love His laugh. It is full of love.

Holy Spirit reveals what the Father wants me to know about the scepter. Do I dare to share the revelation? It will be mocked. It is so precious.

Father draws me back to His Throne. In front of the His Throne is a smaller throne, my size. It matches the scepter in color and material. My humility kicks in and I feel so unworthy. Father won't let unworthiness exist in the Throne Room. I am here by His permission and for His pleasure.

Why Father? Why have you given me the scepter and this throne?

Luke 9:1 Then he called his twelve disciples together, and gave them power and authority over all devils, and to cure diseases.

Father reminds me we are a royal priesthood with God-given power and authority. Rule and reign with Him.

Romans 5:17 For if by one man's offence death reigned by one; much more they which receive abundance of grace and of the gift of righteousness shall reign in life by one, Jesus Christ.

We have our authority all wrong. Our false humility, unsanctified, threatens to make us impotent. We have authority and power through Jesus Christ! I sit on my throne, scepter in hand.

On another trip, Father draws my attention to the other side of the approach. A lake for lack of a better term. It's more like a surface level well with the most beautiful blue water.

I want to dive in, but how deep it is? May I enter the water? Yes comes the answer. I hesitate. I know the water is from God's Throne, the path not visible.

I fall into the water as if I were falling back into bed. I don't sink, but rather, the water catches me, embraces me, caresses me. I don't float, I exist within the water. I can breathe in the water.

Around me I see something, objects, things, ideas, thoughts within the water. My sense of physics is challenged, but I have peace and joy. What is this wonder? This is the water of refreshing. It is refreshing dreams, visions, ideas, provision. What I have yearned for and prayed for is with me in the water.

I know I am bathed in the promises of my Father, soaking in His love, grace and mercy.

I am ready to return to Earth, the revelations mine alone.

10 WHAT DOES HEAVEN LOOK LIKE?

Revelation 21:1
And I saw a new Heaven and a new earth: for the first Heaven and the first earth were passed away; and there was no more sea.

Of course our first and foremost reference for the description of Heaven is the inspired scripture of God. Even what we 'see' in our spiritual vision must not contradict the Word of God. However, Heaven is not limited to what's written in the Word. In John 20:30, we read that Jesus did much more than is written in scripture.

I laugh when I hear someone say, "I don't see it in scripture so I'm not going to do it!'

I tell them, "Well then you better get rid of your car, your cell phone, your microwave, and your television because none of them were in the Bible either."

It is important we remember that as humans, we tend to describe things by what we already know. We are trying to get another person to understand what we see or experience using common knowledge and common language. Since Heaven is anything but common, our descriptions can often fall far short of reality. The old story of blind men describing an elephant comes to mind:

> It was six men of Indostan to learning much inclined,
> Who went to see the Elephant (Though all of them were blind),
> That each by observation might satisfy his mind
>
> The First approached the Elephant, and happening to fall
> Against his broad and sturdy side, at once began to bawl:
> "God bless me! But the Elephant is very like a wall!"
>
> The Second, feeling of the tusk, cried, "Ho! What have we here?
> So very round and smooth and sharp? To me 'tis mighty clear
> This wonder of an Elephant is very like a spear!"
>
> The Third approached the animal, and happening to take
> The squirming trunk within his hands, thus boldly up and spake:
> "I see," quoth he, "the Elephant is very like a snake!"
>
> The Fourth reached out an eager hand, and felt about the knee.
> "What most this wondrous beast is like is mighty plain," quoth he;
> " 'Tis clear enough the Elephant is very like a tree!"
>
> The Fifth, who chanced to touch the ear, said: "E'en the blindest man
> Can tell what this resembles most; deny the fact who can
> This marvel of an Elephant is very like a fan!"
>
> The Sixth no sooner had begun about the beast to grope,
> Then, seizing on the swinging tail that fell within his scope,
> "I see," quoth he, "the Elephant is very like a rope!"
>
> And so these men of Indostan disputed loud and long,
> Each in his own opinion exceeding stiff and strong,
> Though each was partly in the right, and all were in the wrong!
>
> So oft in theologic wars, the disputants, I ween,
> Rail on in utter ignorance of what each other mean,
> And prate about an Elephant not one of them has seen!
>
> American poet John Godfrey Saxe (1816-1887)

Of course the fallacy of this poem is that the blind men might never have seen the objects they used to describe the parts of the elephant.

No man, according to Jesus, had ascended into Heaven save the Son of Man (Himself). By the way, that would include Elijah, folks. That was at that time, but since that time there have been many, many reliable and sane men and women of God like Paul the apostle, who have had the experience(s) of being in Heaven; not just in the Spirit, but actually there. Paul said he didn't know if he was in his body or not when he saw the third Heaven. Since he didn't know; neither do you and I.

Let's, by faith, keep two things in mind . . . these are people describing what they 'saw' in terms with which they are familiar and they may have actually been allowed to visit Heaven temporarily or it may be a spiritual vision from God. Either way, it is the reality of Heaven as we can understand it.

I also want to point out a very important key to understanding the truth in scripture. Look in Daniel 7 beginning in verse 9. "I beheld till the thrones were cast down, and the Ancient of days did sit, Whose garment was white as snow, and the hair of His head like the pure wool: His throne was like the fiery flame, and his wheels as burning fire."

Notice that the English text has words such as, "like", and "as". When Daniel says His garment was white as snow, it certainly doesn't mean the garment was snow or cold, but snow is a color of white with which Daniel is familiar. If a modern day person were seeing this, they might say, "His robe was as white as a neon light on Broadway.

When Daniel describes wheels as burning fire, there weren't wheels with flames on them. In the Hebrew language, wheels is from Strong's 1535, *galgal* which corresponds to Strong's 1534 which is whirlwind (Isaiah 17:13, a rolling thing). In other words there was a supernatural shining or glow swirling around the Ancient of days that looked like fire to Daniel. Perhaps you would describe it as molten lava?

If I were to speak of 'the dew of Heaven' or 'the stars of Heaven', many of you would qualify that by hearing 'dew from Heaven' or 'stars in Heaven'. Dew and stars are part of Heaven we can see with our natural eyes. Dew occurs in Heaven before you can see it. There are many more stars that you and I can see with our natural eyes. Heaven spills over into our existence on earth. It's not a one way street for believers. As the angels descended and ascended Jacob's ladder, so we ascend and descend in and out of Heaven. Stars are in Heaven, from Heaven and of Heaven as is the dew, the rain, the snow.

The Lord asked Job as we read in Job 38:22, "Have you entered into the treasures of the snow?" I ask you, did you think rain and snow are just something that scientifically occur in the atmosphere? Every good and perfect thing comes down from God.

Here's another one for our logical mind to choke on: In Job 38:7 God says the stars sang together! The word sang in the Hebrew language means to give a ringing cry!

Stars—themselves spherical—can produce notes through their vibrations, like musical instruments.

Xi-hydrae, an old star in the constellation Hydra -- It is 130 light years away and 60 times brighter than the Sun. Its sounds, which have been featured in club music in Belgium, are reminiscent of African drumming.
                      Sheffield Hallam University and World Science

Psalm 8:1-4 O LORD, our Lord, how excellent is Your name in all the earth! Who has set Your glory above the Heavens. 2 Out of the mouth of babes and sucklings You have ordained strength because of Your enemies, that You might still the enemy and the avenger. 3 When I consider Your Heavens, the work of Your fingers, the moon and the stars, which You have ordained; 4 What is man, that You are mindful of him? And the son of man, that You visit him?

We traditionally confuse the description of the New Jerusalem seen in Revelation with the description for all of Heaven. That city is just part of the whole. Revelation describes a new Heaven, a new earth and a New Jerusalem.

Heaven is not just streets of gold. Heaven is filled with gold and that gold sometimes spills over into Holy Spirit-filled encounters. Heaven is the place of gemstones, oil, fragrance, light. My husband heard God say in a vision that we are full of 'ultra-<u>violent</u> light'. (The Kingdom of God suffers violence and the violent take it by force.) God's light is powerful! It shines in the darkest darkness and is not overtaken, but dispels darkness.

We have started to refer to the color and light of Heaven as the Aurora Gloryalis rather than the Aurora Borealis.

There are no big lines in the sky where Heaven starts and stops. The space shuttles didn't come across a marker saying, 'Heaven, next left'. God allows us to 'peek' at Heaven from earth, but Heaven is much, much larger and elaborate than we can see or imagine. We must be explorers.

I encourage you to read Job, chapters 38 and 39 in faith, believing God was speaking to Job; that this scriptural account is inspired by God. If you do this, your understanding of creation, including all of Heaven, will be enlarged.

In Malachi, God speaks of opening the windows of Heaven and pouring out a blessing. Windows is actually more of a sluice gate! Don't limit your understanding to an allegory. By faith, know that God is ready to open a portal and dump out blessings over you when you are properly positioned!

Jacob saw a 'ladder' with angels ascending and descending. Do you see a wooden ladder tied together with leather? Did you realize that 'ladder' is highway? Did you know that DNA strands form a ladder?

I have seen angels shoulder to shoulder, wings united swirling in one direction creating a vortex that opened a portal to Heaven and within that vortex there were the colors of Heaven.

Psalm 78:24 And had rained down manna upon them to eat, and had given them of the corn of Heaven.

Psalm 105:40 The people asked, and he brought quails, and satisfied them with the bread of Heaven.

When the children of Israel received the provision of manna and quail and bread, it dropped from the sky above them, but it came out of Heaven from the supply of God. Who do you think made them drop out of the sky? God did it. God dwells in Heaven. From Father's throne, God orchestrates creation on our behalf. Water comes from a rock. Seas part on command. Lightning strikes earth at the word of the prophet. It is our Father who is in Heaven, whose name shall be hallowed. Our Father sits on the Throne of Grace. Our Father bids us to come to Him.

My Father has encouraged me to float in the waters that proceed from the Throne. My Father has let me enter storerooms in Heaven. My Father has assigned angels to take me soaring through the third Heaven!

John 3:27 John answered and said, A man can receive nothing, except it be given him from Heaven.

11 CLOUD OF GLORY

I am driving in my car. The radio is playing some secular station, the GPS is tracking, all is well and normal. Suddenly the GPS 'loses' the signal, then suddenly the radio stops playing and the CD player suddenly takes over. Throne Room Encounters by Joshua Mills begins to play. My spirit man takes over. The thought comes to me, 'concentrate on your driving. Don't close your eyes. Don't close your eyes.' One hand raises in praise, the other on the steering wheel. Why won't the GPS work?

I feel lighter and lighter. Am I being transported. Joshua is singing a spirit song. "In the glory I will stand. . . "

Keep your eyes open. I want to praise with all of me. Keep your eyes on the road. I need to pull over. I can't think. How do I pull over. I am transported. Keep your eyes open.

Joshua is speaking of Ezekiel. I can see what Ezekiel saw. Keep your eyes on the road. The wheel within a wheel. Don't close your eyes. I am flying like Ezekiel. I am in the cloud of glory.

Pull over! I can't. I see what Ezekiel saw. I want to lift both hands. I can't. I'm driving. Oh, the glory!

Breathe. The breath of Heaven. The air is purified in the cloud of glory. Such beauty. Such rapture. Such joy. In the glory I will see every miracle You have for me.

I am back in my vehicle. The CD stops. The radio resumes. The GPS finds the signal. What just happened? Where am I. GPS says I am just where I need to be. Did I close my eyes? How much time has passed? Mere seconds, just minutes.

I am refreshed. This phenomenon happens two more times that day. My vehicle takes on the atmosphere of the Holy Place. Note to self. Listen to the CD at home in the future.

12 WHERE IS HEAVEN?

Gen. 1:8-9 And God called the firmament Heaven.
And the evening and the morning were the second day.
And God said, "Let the waters under the Heaven be
gathered together unto one place, and let the dry land appear:"
and it was so.

Now you may think that 'firmament' sounds like ground, but it's really includes air. God's creation is the supernatural power of God bringing something into natural existence. Our problem in trying to comprehend Heaven is in always considering things from known science which is flawed.

Let's look at the Hebrew word God inspired people to use when writing the story of Creation:

Firmament, Hebrew: raqiya`, pronounced, rä·kē'·ah

Outline of Biblical Usage

    1) extended surface (solid), expanse, firmament

        a) expanse (flat as base, support)

b) firmament (of vault of Heaven supporting waters above)

   2) considered by Hebrews as solid and supporting 'waters' above

Heaven, Hebrew: (plural) shamayim, pronounced, shä·mah'·yim

   1) Heaven, Heavens, sky

      a) visible Heavens, sky

         1) as abode of the stars

         2) as the visible universe, the sky, atmosphere, etc.

      b) Heaven (as the abode of God)[11]

Next we need to consider what scripture actually says instead of mentally filtering through limited human knowledge of how things work.

In Genesis 1:14-15 God said, "Let there be lights in the firmament of the Heaven to divide the day from the night; and let them be for signs, and for seasons, and for days, and Years, and let them be for lights in the firmament of the Heaven to give light upon the earth:" and it was so.

While firmament sounds like ground, it is obviously also the expanse of Heaven and in that firmament are the lights of God.

In Genesis 1:20 God spoke of fowl that may fly above the earth in the open firmament of Heaven.

So Heaven is open above us and is from earth and above. This is the physical, biblical truth of Heaven. This is where we get the idea of looking up at Heaven. Even ancients understood that Heaven was 'up'. There are many verses that describe Heaven as upward.[12]

Gen. 11:4 And they said, Go to, let us build us a city and a tower, whose top may reach unto Heaven ; and let us make us a name, lest

---

[11] www.eliyah.com
[12] Genesis 11:4, 15:5, 28:12, Exodus 9:22, Revelation 21:2

we be scattered abroad upon the face of the whole earth.

Gen. 15:5 And he brought him forth abroad, and said, Look now toward Heaven, and tell the stars, if You be able to number them: and he said unto him, So shall thy seed be.

Gen. 28:12 And he dreamed, and behold a ladder set up on the earth, and the top of it reached to Heaven : and behold the angels of God ascending and descending on it.

In scripture, generally, good things are up and bad things are down. For example one goes down to Egypt and up to Jerusalem.

So we've spoken of the physicality of Heaven, but there are also sections of Heaven.

Consider Deuteronomy 10:14 which tells us of the Heaven of Heavens. Then there's the amazing writing in 2 Corinthians 12:2.

2 Corinthians 12:2 I knew a man in Christ above fourteen years ago, (whether in the body, I cannot tell; or whether out of the body, I cannot tell: God knows;) such an one caught up to the third Heaven.

If there's a third Heaven, then there's at least a first and second Heaven. In a very simplistic outline think of it this way:

First Heaven -   From the ground to the canopy
Second Heaven - From the canopy to the edge of the atmosphere
Third Heaven - Past the atmosphere

Realize that we humans are trying our best to grab clues about Heaven from the source, God's Word, and from revelation in Holy Spirit, it is still imperfect. I think God must laugh at how close we sometimes come to the truth and also how far we miss the reality of Heaven.

I suggest, using a Bible concordance, you heard all the New Testament verses that speak of Heaven or Heavenly places and read them with a receptive Spirit. Let Holy Spirit enlarge your understanding of Heaven.

Revelation 21:1 speaks of a *new* Heaven. If there is a new Heaven, what happens to the old Heaven? It also speaks of a holy Jerusalem descending out of Heaven.

We now live in the Heaven and earth which will pass away at some point. So we're actually studying or exploring a former and a latter Heaven or Heavens.

In scripture, God talks about going 'down' to Egypt which represents a negative environment and 'up' to Jerusalem which represents a positive environment. Up and down are not limited to physical terms, but also refer to source and to God's economy.

I lift up holy hands to honor a high and lofty God. I bow my head and bend my knee to bring earthly existence into subjection to my Holy God.

13 THE MEAL OF MANNA

I rush to return to her bedside. She is old. She is sick. Too soon she will be gone. When I left her she was in a near comatose state, not responding. Will she still be alive?

I enter the room to see her sitting up eating vanilla pudding. I am shocked.

"Is that good?", I ask her as though it were just another day and she had years to live.

"Yes, but not as good as what I had earlier." She continues to bring the spoon to her lips.

"Why, what was the other like?", I ask as I wonder if this is another senile fantasy or is something else afoot. My Spirit is alert. I somehow know to pay special attention to what she says. It is supernatural.

She explains. "It was lighter than this and much better."

"Was it manna?" Where did that idea come from? This is a strange conversation, but I am compelled to listen with spiritual ears.

"Yes, I think it was manna."

"Where did it come from?"

"It came from the table with the hole in the middle." This requires more inquiry.

I discover with further interrogation that she was in a dining hall seated at a large, long table. There were other people there and angels moving about serving, but the food came from an opening in the table. She tells me she'd like more of that food.

I understand. She has seen a vision of Heaven (actually been in Heaven in the Spirit). She had dined at the Master's table. It had refreshed her, rejuvenated her long enough to bear witness.

Within the week she would be gone. She slipped back into a coma inside 24 hours. Was she seeing more wonderful sights? Was she experiencing joys unspeakable?

She was in her mid to late sixties before anyone taught her about God's realm of the Spirit, though saved years before. And now, in her eighties, she was able to slip in and out of Heaven, feasting on manna.

I hear her speaking from inside the trap of the coma. What is she saying? I lean closer. She is praying in her heavenly language. I stay at her bedside singing hymns. Praying in tongues. It is my birthday and I gaze down at this woman who gave me earthly life. We share the eternal life that came from God.

She drifts between the two realms; earth and Heaven. Midnight comes and goes. I whisper in her ear, "Mom, it's not my birthday anymore. It's ok, you can go."

A few more breathes and she goes home perhaps to enjoy more manna. She will fully and eternally access Heaven one day. For now her Spirit makes the journey. Soon, momma, soon . . .

14 YOUR TURN

So I've shared some of my experiences in Heaven with you to give you just an idea what your experiences may be like. Your experience will be unique to you, but heaven is real and you will enjoy the similar places, smells and sounds that many of God's children have enjoyed.

I could fill another book with the many experiences I have had in Heaven and in Heavenly visions, but I prefer you fill your life with your own Heavenly explorations.

I have given you some biblical foundation that demonstrates God's desire and permission for you to enjoy Heaven now. You do not need any human to 'impart' to you what God has already given you. Just access by faith, all that God has in store for you.

By faith, right now, why not go there? Get to a place where you are uninterrupted. Find some nice soaking music and get it started. Turn off your cell phone. Eliminate all the distraction you can. Get comfortable.

Remember, when you start, you might just see nothing, black

nothing, but just wait. The colors will come, the image will form. Holy Spirit will not let you down. You are seeking the Kingdom of God.

Practice this often. The vision and experience will grow and evolve. I am so excited for you. It's glorious to visit Father's house.

Now, in a moment you are going to put down this book, close your eyes and relax and soar into Heaven.

Here is a prayer to help you get started.

Father God, I am your child for I confess Jesus as Lord and believe in my heart that you raised Jesus from the dead. I ask you now to reveal to me what you would like me to experience about Heaven. I bind all interference of the enemy, the devil and I release Holy Spirit power into my time with You, in the name of Jesus.

Be still.

There it is . . .

ABOUT THE AUTHOR

Dr. Linda Smith – Christian, pastor, teacher, author, minister and wife. In partnership with her husband, Robert, she co-founded Free Them Ministries, Inc., an international Christian outreach. Together they also pastor PowerHouse Christian Center in San Marcos, Texas. Dr. Smith was ordained into the ministry of Jesus Christ in 1981 with a directive from God to set the captives free from their pasts, their false assumptions concerning God and His word, and the emotional barriers that have been placed between people and God.

With an earned Ph.D. in Theology, and a gift for teaching, Linda presents the dynamic word of God in a way that personalizes the message for the hearer. Students come away from Dr. Smith's classes with an excitement for the word of God and an ability to find out for themselves the meaning of the scriptures. Dr. Smith has served the church for over thirty years educating people of all ages with the Word of God. She has also served on the faculty board of Christian universities and was the Christian Education Director in several churches across America.

Linda uses the Bible, humor and her testimony to exhort the people of God seek a more intimate walk with the Lord Jesus Christ. Her ministry is a mandate to create spiritual maturity and integrity in churches, businesses and homes with anointed messages that glorify God Almighty. This minister of God is Holy Spirit filled and has a sincere desire in her heart for the Bride of Christ to be fully prepared for marriage to the Bridegroom.

www.ingramcontent.com/pod-product-compliance
Lightning Source LLC
Chambersburg PA
CBHW061344040426
42444CB00011B/3073